This book belongs to:

A Treasury for Five Year Olds

A Treasury for Five Year Olds

A Collection of Stories, Fairy Tales and Nursery Rhymes

p

Language Consultant: Betty Root.

This is a Parragon book
This edition published in 2006

Parragon
Queen Street House
4 Queen Street
Bath BA1 1HE, UK

Printed in China

1-40546-943-9

✦ *Contents* ✦

The Emperor's New Clothes

A long time ago, there lived an emperor who loved clothes. He loved them so much that he spent all his money on them. He had a different suit for every hour of the day. He cared about nothing else.

One day, two dishonest men came to the emperor's kingdom. They said that they could weave the finest cloth in the whole world. The cloth would be so fine that it would be invisible to anyone who was either stupid or not good enough to do their job.

The rumours about these men soon reached the ears of the emperor.

"I must have some of that cloth," he thought. "Not only will it make me look splendid, but it will also help me find out which of my men are stupid or not good enough for their job."

So the two rogues were invited to the emperor's palace. They set up their looms and were soon hard at work pretending to weave the cloth. They asked for the very finest silks and the purest gold and silver thread. Of course, these materials all went straight into the rogues' bags. This was all one big joke – there is no such thing as invisible cloth.

The emperor was keen to see how the weavers were

getting on, but he was also afraid. What if he saw nothing? Would that mean he was stupid? Would that mean he was unfit to be emperor? Before visiting them, he decided to send his first minister. He was such a clever man that he was sure to see the cloth.

When the first minister entered the room where the two men were weaving, he looked and looked but could see nothing. "Gracious," he thought. "Does this mean I'm stupid? Does this mean I'm unfit to do my job? No one must know. I will pretend that I've seen the cloth."

Then he listened very carefully as the rogues described all the fine patterns and colours in the cloth. Later, the first minister repeated their words to the emperor.

When he heard how magnificent the cloth was, the emperor decided to see for himself. He took all his ministers, including the first minister, and entered the weaving room.

The emperor looked and looked but, to his dismay, he could see nothing. "Oh, my!" he thought. "Does this mean I'm stupid, or does it mean I'm unfit to be emperor? Either way, nobody must ever know." And so, he too decided to pretend that he could see the invisible cloth.

"Wonderful! Marvellous!" he cried out loud. As the first minister pointed out this colour and that design, the other ministers looked and looked but, of course, they could see nothing. None of

them dared admit to being stupid or unfit for their job, so they also praised the cloth. "It's beautiful," said one. "You really should have some clothes made from it for your annual procession," advised another.

The emperor soon agreed and the two weavers set to work and pretended to make a fine suit for the emperor. They worked long into the night on the days before the procession. They waved scissors here and needles there. Everyone was very impressed because the two rogues worked so hard.

Finally, the day of the procession arrived. The whole city was talking about the emperor's new suit. People couldn't wait to see it for themselves. More importantly, they couldn't wait to see which of their friends and neighbours could see it, and which of them could not, proving they were either stupid or unfit for their job. The whole city was buzzing.

The suit itself was ready just in time.

"The cloth is as light as a feather. It's so light that you could almost imagine you were wearing nothing," explained one of the rogues.

Then he helped the emperor into first the trousers, then the jacket.

"I'm sure you'll agree that the suit is magnificent," said the other rogue, making the emperor, who was really quite naked, twirl around in front of the mirror.

The emperor turned this way and that, trying to see if he could catch the merest glimpse of the suit. But it was no good, he could still see nothing. Aloud he said, "It's splendid. Quite the finest suit I own."

"Yes, splendid," agreed his first minister. "You've never looked more royal."

The emperor did not want anyone to know that he was unfit to do his job. Convinced that he was, indeed, dressed in a most splendid suit, the emperor held his head up high and went to join his procession.

As he marched through the street, all the people watching cried out, "Just look at the emperor's new clothes. They are the most beautiful we have ever seen."

No one would admit that they could not see the clothes. They were afraid that if they did, everyone would know they were either stupid or unfit for their job.

Then, at last, a child pushed to the front of the crowd and began to point at the emperor and laugh.

"But the emperor's got nothing on," he giggled.

A ripple went through the crowd. Suddenly, everyone knew that the child was right. There was the proud emperor walking naked through the streets of the city. Everyone began to point at him and laugh.

Even the emperor knew that they were right. But he did nothing for fear of looking even more stupid. He just carried on walking and pretended he was wearing his favourite suit. Wasn't he a silly emperor?

Hansel and Grethel

There was once a poor woodcutter, who lived in the forest with his wife and two children, called Hansel and Grethel. The woodcutter loved Hansel and Grethel dearly, but his wife felt quite differently about them. She was their stepmother, and wished they had never been born.

One cold winter, there was not enough food in the woodcutter's house, and everyone was hungry. One night, after the children had gone to bed, the stepmother said to her husband, "Something has to be done, or we will all starve.

Tomorrow you must take the children into the wood and leave them there."

"No," gasped the woodcutter. "I couldn't do such an evil thing to them."

But the wicked stepmother wouldn't leave the woodcutter alone until he had agreed. Luckily for Hansel and Grethel, they heard their stepmother's wicked plan.

"What shall we do?" sobbed Grethel.

"Don't worry," said Hansel, who had been looking out of the window. "I have an idea." He slipped out into the garden, put a handful of white pebbles into his pocket and then crept back to bed.

The following morning, Hansel and Grethel followed the woodcutter and his wife deep into the forest. Along the way Hansel kept stopping to drop a pebble onto the ground.

When they reached the middle of the forest, the woodcutter made a fire and told the children he would return at the end of the day. Of course, he never did.

Night fell, and strange sounds filled the forest.

"How shall we find our way home?" sobbed Grethel.

"Don't worry," said Hansel. "Wait until the Moon rises."

When, at last, the Moon began to shine, the white pebbles twinkled like stars. As Hansel had planned, they followed the pebbles all the way home. The woodcutter was overjoyed at his children's safe return.

Shortly after, the family had even less food in the house. Again, the children heard their stepmother say to their father, "Tomorrow you must take the children farther into the wood and leave them."

After much argument, their father agreed. When they had gone to sleep, Hansel tried to go outside to collect some pebbles, but his stepmother had locked the door.

The following morning, the children were each given a crust of bread and told to follow their father into the forest. As he walked, Hansel dropped breadcrumbs behind him.

Eventually, their father led them to a different part of the forest. "I'll be back when I've finished work," said the woodcutter. Of course, he never returned.

"Don't worry," Hansel said to Grethel. "When the Moon rises, we will be able to follow the breadcrumbs home."

However, when the Moon rose there were no breadcrumbs. The birds of the forest had eaten them. Hansel and Grethel wandered in the forest all night long, but they got more and more lost. Eventually, they grew so tired that they lay down to sleep.

In the morning, the children walked deeper into the forest until they came to a little cottage. It was made of bread, cakes and sweets! Hansel and Grethel were so hungry that they began to break bits off to eat. Suddenly, the door swung open and out burst a witch.

"Gotcha, you nasty nippers," she cackled, grabbing Hansel and Grethel. "You think you can scoff my house, do you? We'll just see how you like being eaten." Then she dragged the children into her cottage and threw Hansel into a cage. "When he's big and fat, I'm going to eat him. Ha, ha, ha, ha!"

Over the next weeks, the witch gave the very finest food to Hansel, but she gave Grethel only scraps and bones. Grethel gave one of these bones to her brother. "Hold it when the witch asks for a finger to feel how fat you are," said Grethel. "She is so blind that she won't know the difference."

Grethel was right, and the witch was amazed that Hansel did not grow fatter. Then, one day, she could wait no longer.

"Fat or thin, I'm going to eat him," she cackled. "Light the oven, Grethel."

Weeping, poor Grethel did as she was told. Soon the fire

beneath the oven was blazing.

"Is it hot enough yet?" asked the witch, who was beginning to grow hungry.

"I don't know," said Grethel. "How can you tell?"

"Out of my way, you stupid girl," growled the witch. She pushed Grethel aside and stuck her head in the oven. Quick as a flash, Grethel pushed the evil witch into the oven and slammed the door shut.

Grethel quickly found the witch's keys and released Hansel. Then they used the keys to open all the chests in the witch's cottage. Inside they found gold, silver and precious stones.

"Father should be able to buy all the food we need with this," said Hansel, filling his pockets.

Once more, the children set off in search of home. They walked through the forest for a long time. Then, at last they came to a place they knew and were able to find their father's cottage. Their father, whose wife had left him, was overjoyed to see them. His happiness was even greater when he saw the treasures that Hansel and Grethel had brought.

"Aaah! We need never go hungry again," he cried, hugging Hansel and Grethel. And from that day, they knew nothing but happiness.

The House That Jack Built

This is the house that Jack built.

This is the malt
That lay in the house that Jack built.

This is the rat,
That ate the malt
That lay in the house that Jack built.

This is the cat,
That killed the rat,
That ate the malt
That lay in the house that Jack built.

This is the dog,
That worried the cat,
That killed the rat,
That ate the malt
That lay in the house that Jack built.

This is the cow with the crumpled horn,
That tossed the dog,
That worried the cat,
That killed the rat,
That ate the malt
That lay in the house that Jack built.

This is the maiden all forlorn,
That milked the cow with the crumpled horn,
That tossed the dog,
That worried the cat,
That killed the rat,
That ate the malt
That lay in the house that Jack built.

This is the man all tattered and torn,
That kissed the maiden all forlorn,
That milked the cow with the crumpled horn,
That tossed the dog,
That worried the cat,
That killed the rat,
That ate the malt
That lay in the house that Jack built.

This is the priest all shaven and shorn,
That married the man all tattered and torn,
That kissed the maiden all forlorn,
That milked the cow with the crumpled horn,
That tossed the dog,
That worried the cat,
That killed the rat,
That ate the malt
That lay in the house that Jack built.

This is the cock that crowed in the morn,
That waked the priest all shaven and shorn,
That married the man all tattered and torn,
That kissed the maiden all forlorn,
That milked the cow with the crumpled horn,
That tossed the dog,
That worried the cat,
That killed the rat,
That ate the malt
That lay in the house that Jack built.

Frieda Gets Her Wings

Frieda was the tiniest fairy in the glade, smaller than all her friends. She was more shy and timid, too – in fact, everything seemed to frighten Frieda. When Frieda heard something go "Flap-flutter-flap! Flap-flutter-flap!" she ran to hide among the daffodils.

"Come out, silly!" laughed her friend Felicity. "It's only a butterfly!" Frieda's cheeks turned bright pink with embarrassment.

"Splish-splosh! Splish-splosh!" Frieda heard, as she felt something wet on her head.

"Oh, no!" she quavered, ducking under a toadstool.

"It's just a little rain!" laughed Wendy and Melissa.

"How can you be frightened of that?" Frieda turned away, ashamed.

"Whoooooosh! Whoooooooosh!" Frieda heard, and she rushed to shelter inside a hollow log.

"Frieda's even afraid of the wind!" said Wendy. "She'll never get her fairy wings!"

A tiny tear slipped out of Frieda's eye. More frightening than the wind, or the rain, or the butterfly's flapping wings, was the thought that Wendy might be right. Frieda longed to get her fairy wings – she dreamed of the day when she would be able to flitter and fly in the moonlight like the grown-up fairies. But she knew that she would have to earn those wings.

Every year on the first day of spring, the Fairy Queen gave lacy, delicate wings to all the young fairies who

had proved their bravery. Any fairy who wasn't truly brave would have to wait for another whole year.

Frieda was hoping that it would be her turn this year. But how could a frightened fairy ever be brave?

As the first day of spring drew near, all the young fairies tried to outdo one another with daring deeds. From her golden throne beside the glade, the Fairy Queen watched them all.

Frieda watched too.

"I can reach the top of the rosebush!" Melissa called, climbing up the thorny stem. Waving proudly from the top, she plucked a perfect blossom. Then she leapt down with it and raced to the Fairy Queen's throne.

"A present for you, Your Majesty," said Melissa, curtseying before the Queen. "I didn't mind the thorns, and I wasn't even frightened when I jumped

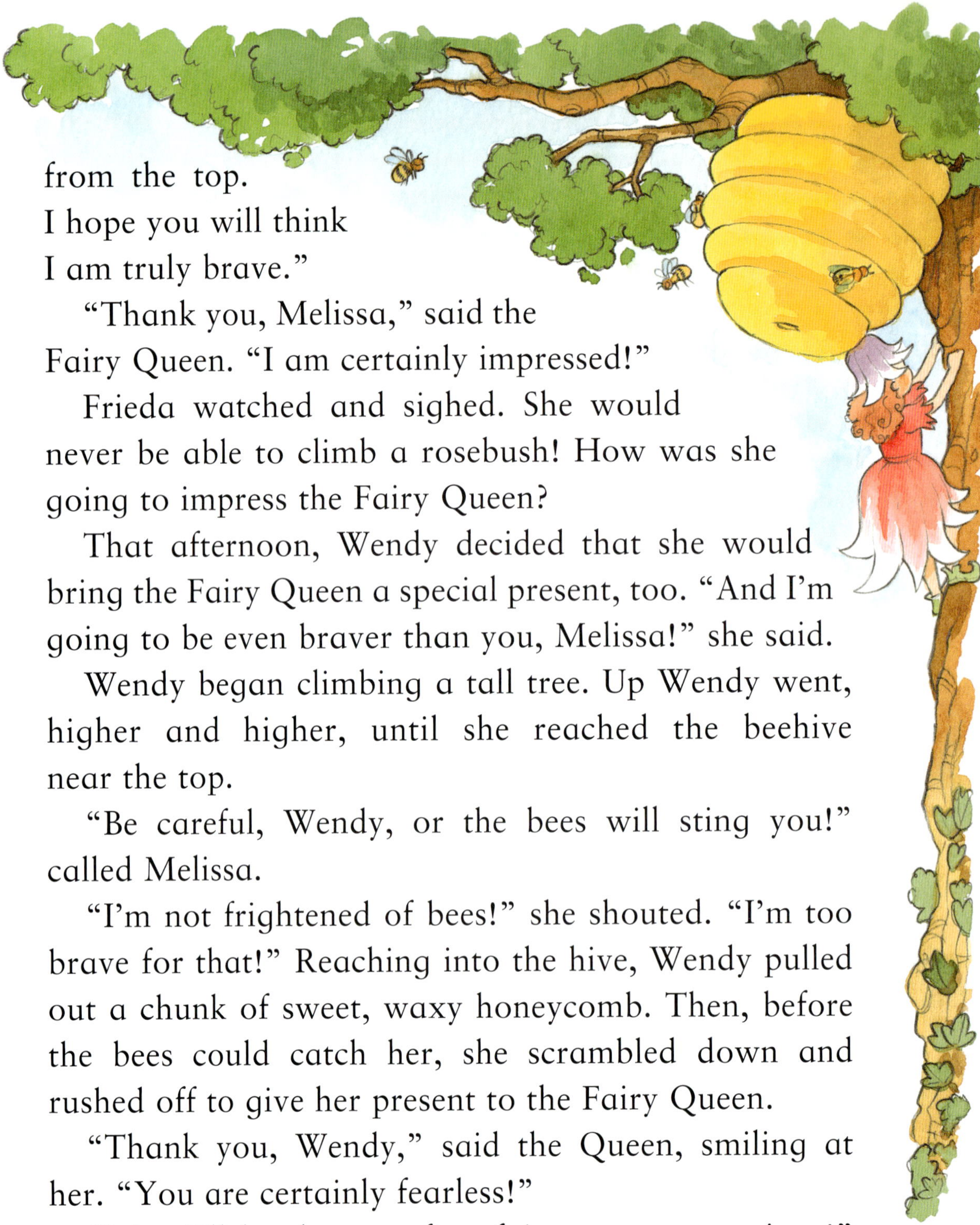

from the top.
I hope you will think
I am truly brave."

"Thank you, Melissa," said the Fairy Queen. "I am certainly impressed!"

Frieda watched and sighed. She would never be able to climb a rosebush! How was she going to impress the Fairy Queen?

That afternoon, Wendy decided that she would bring the Fairy Queen a special present, too. "And I'm going to be even braver than you, Melissa!" she said.

Wendy began climbing a tall tree. Up Wendy went, higher and higher, until she reached the beehive near the top.

"Be careful, Wendy, or the bees will sting you!" called Melissa.

"I'm not frightened of bees!" she shouted. "I'm too brave for that!" Reaching into the hive, Wendy pulled out a chunk of sweet, waxy honeycomb. Then, before the bees could catch her, she scrambled down and rushed off to give her present to the Fairy Queen.

"Thank you, Wendy," said the Queen, smiling at her. "You are certainly fearless!"

"I bet I'll be the very first fairy to get my wings!"

Wendy boasted to her friends.

The next day, as Frieda and her friends played in the wood, a dragonfly zoomed past. Frieda ran to hide, but Melissa chased after it.

"See how brave I am!" she shouted, leaping on to the dragonfly's back. "I'm not afraid of anything!"

"Zooom! Vrooom!" went the dragonfly, swooping and looping and soaring through the air.

"Yipppeeee!" cried Melissa. "Being brave is fun!" The Fairy Queen watched closely and smiled. But Frieda, standing by herself, was miserable.

"I can't climb high, and I'm scared of dragonflies," she thought. "How will I ever earn my wings?"

Suddenly, Frieda's thoughts were interrupted by a noise coming from a puddle behind her. Frieda turned to listen. It was someone crying for help!

Frieda ran over and saw a ladybird struggling in the water. "Help me, please!" she called. "I can't swim!"

The ladybird would drown unless someone dived in to save her. But Frieda's friends were all watching Melissa and the dragonfly. Frieda was the only one who could help!

"Don't be scared!" said Frieda, trying to stop her voice from trembling. "I'm coming to get you!"

Quaking with fear, Frieda jumped into the puddle and swam out to the ladybird.

"Climb on my back," she said to the grateful little bug.

All at once Melissa saw what was happening.

"Look!" she told the others. "Frieda is rescuing a ladybird!" They all ran over to watch, and they cheered as Frieda brought the ladybird to safety. Fluttering above them all, the Fairy Queen looked down and smiled.

The next day was the first day of spring, and all the fairies, young and old, gathered before the Fairy Queen's throne to see who would get their wings today. The young fairies were chattering with excitement.

"Hush!" said one of the older fairies. "The Queen is ready to make her announcement!"

"All the young fairies have been bold and daring," said the Fairy Queen, "and they should all feel proud. But only one fairy has shown true bravery, so I will give only one pair of wings today, and that fairy is Frieda. It was easy for the others to be brave, because they aren't afraid of anything. But Frieda did something very brave although she was afraid. Frieda, come forward."

To the sound of cheers and applause, Frieda made her way through the crowd. As she knelt down, the

Fairy Queen waved her wand, sending out a shower of glittering fairy dust. There were gasps of delight as a pair of shimmering, lacy silver wings appeared on Frieda's shoulders.

Frieda's friends rushed over to look at her new wings.

"I'm sorry we laughed at you," said Melissa quietly.

"Me too," said Wendy. "Now I can see that you're the bravest of us all."

"Thank you," said Frieda, smiling. Then, very gently, she fluttered her brand-new wings and rose into the air above the admiring crowd. Frieda's dream had come true at last.

The Owl and the Pussycat

The Owl and the Pussycat went to sea
In a beautiful pea-green boat,
They took some honey, and plenty of money,
Wrapped up in a five-pound note.

The Owl looked up to the stars above,
And sang to a small guitar,
"O lovely Pussy! O Pussy, my love,
What a beautiful Pussy, you are,
You are,
You are!
What a beautiful Pussy, you are!"

Pussy said to the Owl, "You elegant fowl!
How charmingly sweet you sing!
O let us be married, too long we have tarried:
But what shall we do for a ring?"

They sailed away for a year and a day,
To the land where the Bong-tree grows
And there in a wood a Piggy-wig stood
With a ring at the end of his nose,
His nose,
His nose,
With a ring at the end of his nose.

“Dear Pig, are you willing to sell for one shilling
Your ring?” Said the Piggy, “I will.”
So they took it away and were married next day
By the Turkey who lives on the hill.

They dined on mince, and slices of quince,
Which they ate with a runcible spoon;
And hand in hand, on the edge of the sand,
They danced by the light of the moon,
The moon,
The moon,
They danced by the light of the moon.

Hopalong Hopscotch

Hopscotch really loved his book of fairy stories. Above all, he loved the story of the frog who was kissed by a beautiful princess.

"He became a handsome prince," said Hopscotch. "That sounds fun."

Hopscotch showed the story to his friend Polly.

"I'm off to find a princess to kiss," said Hopscotch. Polly liked Hopscotch a lot. They had been friends since they were tadpoles.

"Don't go," she said. " Have a slice of fly pie instead."

"No thanks," he replied. "I'm going to hop along to find a princess."

With his fairy book in the basket on the front of his tricycle, Hopscotch pedalled past the lily pond and the rest of his family.

"The fly pie is fantastic today," said Polly. But Hopscotch simply smiled.

Hopscotch headed over the hill, steered under a bridge and sped round a corner past three big toads on bicycles.

"Look at him!" said the biggest toad to the other two. But Hopscotch didn't notice them because he had caught sight of a princess. She was carrying her shopping out of a car.

"Ah ha! Time for a kiss," thought Hopscotch.

He left his tricycle and hopped over to the princess excitedly. She saw the frog's large smiling lips ready for a kiss.

"EEEEEK!" screamed the princess.

Her carrier bags shot up into the air; her shopping flew everywhere. One bag split apart, showering flour over the three big toads. They had followed Hopscotch

on their bicycles.

WHAP! WHOOPS! WALLOP! The toads crashed into each other, but Hopscotch didn't even notice.

"EEEK! EEEEEK!" the princess screamed even louder, speeding into her palace with Hopscotch hopping along behind her. She slammed the door in his face.

"That wasn't much fun!" moaned Hopscotch as he pedalled home, down Long Lane. He didn't even notice the three toads, blotched with flour, behind him near the railway line. In Midsummer Wood Hopscotch saw a second princess. She was picking some flowers.

"Come on, Hopscotch. Hopalong!" He pedalled faster. Suddenly, from behind a tree, came a terrible sound. WOOF! WOOF! WOOF! A huge dog hurtled towards Hopscotch.

Turning his tricycle, Hopscotch swerved and skidded through a dirty puddle. He just missed a mole on roller-skates. The barking dog was catching Hopscotch up.

"Oh dear! Oh dear!" Hopscotch pedalled quickly round a tree.

THUMP! His tricycle hit a fallen branch.

WHEEE! Hopscotch looped the loop and fell onto his back. A shiny black nose came closer . . . and closer . . .

and closer. SPLISH! A large pink tongue came closer . . . and closer . . . and closer.

"Banjo! Here Banjo!" a voice shouted. Banjo the dog stopped, turned and bounded off.

"That wasn't much fun!" said Hopscotch as he trudged back to his tricycle. He cycled away from Midsummer Wood and through a field by a winding stream. There he saw a third princess.

"Hello!" he said. "I'm Hopalong Hopscotch."

The princess greeted Hopscotch with a great big smile, which spread across her face. "What a pet!" she said picking him up. "Cute and nicely green."

Hopscotch got his lips ready for a really magic kiss. But the princess popped him into a large glass jar and screwed the lid on tight.

"Hey!" called Hopscotch. "This isn't right!"

"It certainly isn't!" said a small toad sitting beside him. "She pulled me off my bicycle this morning and I've been in here ever since!"

Suddenly, the princess

tripped over a branch lying on the path. The glass jar went flying through the air.

WHOOOOOOOOOSH!

"Help!" yelped Hopscotch.

"Hold on!" cried the small toad.

The jar splashed into the stream and smashed into pieces. The small toad and Hopscotch swam to the bank.

"Look! My toad friends are coming to help me," said the small toad.

"WHERE ARE MY PETS?" screamed the princess. The small toad jumped onto the biggest toad's bicycle. Then, waving to Hopscotch, they speedily rode off.

"That wasn't much fun!" moaned Hopscotch as he quickly pedalled back to the lily pond.

In front of the blackberry bushes a princess on a skateboard stopped beside him. Before he could

say "Hopalong Hopscotch" the princess kissed him on the cheek.

"That was fun!" she said smiling.

"Yes, but I'm not a handsome prince," moaned Hopscotch.

"Never mind!" replied the princess. And taking off her disguise, 'princess' Polly laughed.

"You kissed me as a princess and now you're a frog!" laughed Hopscotch.

"Would you like another kiss?" asked Polly.

"I'd rather have a piece of fly pie," answered Hopscotch, and together they hopped happily home.

The Little Mermaid

Long ago, deep below the ocean blue, there lay the kingdom of the mer-people. The mer-people were similar to humans, but instead of legs they had tails like fish. At the centre of the kingdom stood the mer-king's splendid palace. Inside the palace lived the mer-king, his mother and his six mermaid daughters. The six princesses were all beautiful, but the youngest was the fairest of them all. She was also blessed with the sweetest of voices.

The little mermaid loved to hear about the human world. She would spend many hours listening to her grandmother's stories about sailors and their huge ships, about busy towns and animals that walked on the land.

"When you are fifteen," said her grandmother, "you will be allowed to go to the surface of the sea, and see all these things for yourself."

Year after year, the little mermaid looked on as her sisters reached their fifteenth birthday. One by one, each mermaid made her first journey to the water's surface.

At last, the little mermaid's fifteenth birthday arrived. As she rose to the water's surface, she saw a large ship at anchor. Its decks were alive with men dancing and singing noisily. Among the men was a handsome prince. It was

his sixteenth birthday and the whole ship was celebrating.

The little mermaid watched the handsome prince late into the night. Then the ocean began to bubble and swirl. A storm arrived, and the big ship was tossed from wave to wave.

Suddenly, the ship was thrown onto its side and began to sink. The little mermaid realized that the men were in danger, but it was so dark that she could not see what was happening. As the ship plunged below the waves, the little mermaid spotted the unconscious body of the prince. Ignoring the danger, she swam to his side and caught hold of him.

The mermaid swam and swam until she reached the nearest shore. She dragged the prince onto a sandy beach and then slipped back into the sea and waited.

Early the next morning, a group of young girls came out of a large white building by the beach to walk along the water's edge. Before long, one of the younger girls found the prince. She knelt beside him as he began to wake up. How the little mermaid's heart ached as the prince smiled up at the young girl. He thought it was she, and not the little mermaid, who had saved him. The little mermaid felt so sad that she plunged beneath the waves and returned home.

Day by day, the little mermaid became more and more unhappy. At last, she revealed her secret to one of her sisters. Soon all the other mermaids knew her story.

Luckily, one of them knew where the prince lived, and was happy to show the little mermaid the way to his palace by the sea.

After the little mermaid had found her prince's palace, she used to return there most evenings. Hidden by darkness, she would watch him from the water as he stood on his balcony overlooking the sea. The prince grew more and more dear to the little mermaid. However, she knew that he could never love her, for to be admired by a human she needed two legs instead of a tail.

One day, the little mermaid decided she would risk everything to win the prince's love. So she went to visit an evil witch.

"I know what you want," cackled the witch. "I will prepare you a drink that will give you legs instead of a tail. However, whenever you walk it will feel as if you are walking on broken glass.

Do you agree to this?"

"Yes!" cried the princess.

"If the prince marries another, your heart will break and you will turn into foam on the sea," added the witch. "It will be as if you never existed. Also, you must pay me with your voice."

"But how will I charm the prince without my voice?" asked the little mermaid.

"What do I care?" cried the witch. So the little mermaid gave away her voice in return for the witch's potion. Unable to speak or sing, she headed to the prince's palace. Once there, she drank the witch's potion. She felt it run through her body like sharp knives, and then she fell down in a swoon.

When the little mermaid awoke, her tail had been replaced with legs. She stood up to walk and found that the witch had been right – every step felt as if she was walking on

broken glass. However, when she came across the prince, she forgot her pain. The prince asked the little mermaid who she was but, of course, she could not speak.

The prince was delighted with the little mermaid, and took her with him everywhere he went. However, he looked upon her as a sweet child and never thought of making her his wife. He would tell her how he wished to marry a young girl who had saved his life after a shipwreck. “I saw her only once,” he would say, “but she is the only one I can ever love. She is the girl I wish to marry.” The little mermaid was unable to tell him that she was the one who had saved his life.

One day, the prince's parents arranged for him to sail to a neighbouring kingdom to marry a princess. “Don't worry,” he told the mermaid. “I must go but it is impossible for me to love her. If I cannot have the girl I love, I will marry you.”

However, when the prince saw the princess, he cried out, “It is her! She is the one who saved my life.” It was decided that they should marry without delay.

The little mermaid was very sad. As she watched the prince and his bride marry, she wept silent tears. Later, after everyone else was asleep, her sisters appeared. They had lost their beautiful golden hair, and their heads were shaved bare.

"We have made a deal with the witch," said the eldest sister. "We have given her our hair in return for this knife. If you plunge it into the prince's heart, you will become a mermaid again."

The little mermaid loved the prince so dearly that she could never think of taking his life. Throwing the knife aside, she leapt into the ocean. However, instead of dissolving into foam, she found herself floating gently upwards. Around her were many beautiful wispy shapes. Then she saw that she too was like them. The little mermaid had been so sweet and good that she had earned herself a place in heaven.

The Sad Dragon

Dotty Dragon was unhappy. This morning had not started well. She had fallen out of a tree, which is a horrid way to begin the day.

Dotty had been dreaming; she was sliding down a grassy slope, faster and faster, until suddenly she crashed into a sharp, spiky tree.

"Ow! I don't like this dream!" shouted Dotty Dragon, waking up with a jolt.

Only it wasn't a dream at all now. It was real. Dotty had tumbled out of her nest in the Silver Tree and was dropping down through the spiky branches.

Why, you might ask, didn't Dotty simply fly back up again? The trouble is that although dragons are excellent flyers, they do need to warm up first. They have to flap their wings and stretch their necks before take-off.

However, there is no time to flap and stretch when you are asleep. So Dotty just fell – fast and hard. She landed with a big bump that woke all the other dragons in the forest.

"Ssssh!" shouted the dragons. "Don't make so much noise!"

Poor Dotty was covered in red bumps and purple bruises. And, to make matters even worse, her fire breath would not light.

"All that banging and bumping must have put out my fire!" sighed Dotty as she tried desperately to make a flame.

It was early morning. The air was cold. Dotty shivered; she felt miserable. She needed her flame to warm her up – and to cook her breakfast of fried eggs.

Dotty tried again to blow fire. She huffed and puffed. She panted and wheezed. She opened her jaws wide. She blew through tiny puckered lips. But nothing worked.

Her flame had vanished.

Big tears slid down Dotty's long nose.

Now you may not know this, but dragons cry like fountains. They have lots of water inside their bodies so that if their flames start a surprise fire, they can put it out like a fire engine. Soon Dotty was sitting in a lake of tears, and her sobs woke the other dragons again.

"Whatever is the matter?" demanded Danny.

"Why are you crying?" asked Flame.

"You do look funny," said Spike. "You are covered in red bumps and purple bruises."

"I fell out of the tree," sobbed Dotty.

"I am sore all over and now my flame won't work."

"That's not surprising," said Spike. "With all that water flowing down your face, no flame could ever light up."

"It's all right for you," Dotty shouted into the trees. "You're all still cosy in your nests. I am hungry and cold." And Dotty stomped off into the forest.

"Come back!" called her friends. "We might be able to help."

But Dotty just stomped even harder and faster. She was in a very bad mood indeed. When she reached the edge of the Purple Mountains, she sat down on a pile of yellow boulders to sulk.

"Are you all right?" asked a shrill, piping voice.

"No! I am not all right. I am all wrong!" answered Dotty. "Go away!"

"I only want to help," said

a sleek blue raven, flying down to perch beside her.

Dotty sniffed. She gulped. She tried not to cry but one big tear began to trickle and tickle down her wrinkly face.

"Oh dear," said the raven. "You are unhappy."

"I have lost my flame," Dotty sobbed, "and nobody cares."

"I care," said the raven.

"Huh!" snapped Dotty. "I am cold, and I can't fry my eggs for breakfast. Nobody understands."

More tears began to gush.

"I understand," said the raven, ". . . and I think I can help. I know just the place to find a new flame."

"Really!" gulped Dotty, staring at him. "Where?"

The raven hopped onto Dotty's knobbly nose. "You have to promise not to cry any more so your face can dry out – and promise to be in a better mood."

"Okay," sighed Dotty, "I'll try."

"Right," went on the raven. "At the top of this mountain lives the Phoenix. He is a magic bird made of fire, and has the most beautiful crimson and gold flames that you have ever seen."

"Wow!" said Dotty, blinking back the last tear.

"Yes," said the raven. "And I am sure that if you ask him politely, he will spare you one little flicker of fire to light your flame."

"Wow!" said Dotty again.

Then Dotty and the raven set off up the mountainside.

It took them a while to fly right to the top. And when they arrived, there was the Phoenix dancing in the sunset. He was beautiful, and he glowed and flickered with flame.

"I have been expecting you," called the Phoenix. "Come closer."

Dotty stepped up, feeling nervous. Then the Phoenix smiled and said, "Dotty, the greatest warmth comes from friendship. Your flame is still there but it needs you to believe in yourself – and in your friends. Go back and be kind to all the other little dragons. Be happy – and in no time at all, your flame will return."

So that is what Dotty did. With the raven perched on her shoulder, she flew down the mountain, through the forest and back to her Silver Tree. Dawn was just turning the sky pink with the new day.

"Hello, Dotty," called Danny.

"It is good to see you back," cried Flame.

"We have missed you," added Spike.

"Welcome home," chorused her friends.

"Thank you," replied Dotty. Then she smiled. And as she smiled, she felt her fire begin to glow again, deep in her throat, warm and wonderful.

Then, suddenly, a bright flame burst out of her mouth. It burned with a warm glow.

"Today is going to be perfect," said Dotty, grinning from ear to ear as her bright flames – and her friends – danced all around her.

Little Duck Has Big Ideas

Little Duck was born one springtime near a gurgling, sparkling river. Little Duck loved her river. She loved to travel up and down it, among the other white ducks, the great, white swans and the beautiful, many-coloured wild ducks. Sometimes, she went exploring, swimming hard upstream, and then she let the river carry her back to her home in the rustling reeds.

Little Duck had so many friends along this river! The rabbits popped up from their burrows in the hillside to wave at Little Duck, or suddenly popped out at her from behind a gorse bush.

"Rabbitrabbitrabbit!" cried the rabbits.

"Quack, quack!" answered Little Duck.

Farther downstream lived a family of field mice. Little Duck liked to see if she could spot a mouse baby peeping shyly from beneath a dockleaf.

"Quack, quack!" called Little Duck.

"Squeek-eek-eek!" answered the mouse baby. Past the meadow were the woods where the squirrels played. Little Duck quacked and quacked to cheer them on.

At last she would glide into her rustly home in the reeds, where the frogs croaked out their songs to her at night.

"Croak, croak, home you are," they called.

The river was a happy, crowded place in summer. Little Duck especially loved to watch the wild ducks. She remembered the day they arrived, back in the springtime. There was a rush and whirr of

wings, and down came all these beautiful strangers out of nowhere. But now it was autumn, and the leaves were falling. The air turned colder.

"It's time to leave," said the leader of the wild ducks.

"You're going to leave the river?" asked Little Duck.

"Oh yes. Nobody wants to stay here for the winter. We're flying south."

"South!" thought Little Duck. "Oh," she cried, "I want to come with you. I want to fly!"

"Then come along!" said the wild duck. "You're very welcome."

Little Duck went off to tell all her friends.

"I've come to say goodbye!" she said, importantly. "I'm flying south!"

"Oh, don't go away!" cried all her friends. "Don't go away and leave our lovely river!"

But Little Duck replied, "Nobody wants to stay here for the winter."

The next day, the wild ducks gathered close again.

"Come along!" they cried, "It's time to go!" And Little Duck went with them.

Up, up, up flew the wild ducks. Up, up, up flew Little Duck. They made one great, wonderful swoop all round the sky.

And then, Little Duck looked down at the rabbit hill and the mousey meadow, the squirrel wood and the rustly reed bed. There was her lovely river, winding round them. And it was all getting smaller and smaller every minute.

Little Duck looked up at the great big empty sky. She looked down at her old home, and realized that she didn't want to leave it after all.

"Goodbye!" she called to the wild ducks. "I'm going back home again!"

WHOOOSH! Down, down, down swooped Little Duck, and SPLASH! There she was again, home at last in the river.

"Here I am! I'm home!" cried Little Duck.

"Who are you?" asked the rabbits and the field mice, the squirrels and the frogs. "We don't think we know you."

"I am your friend, Little Duck!" said Little Duck.

"Oh no," they said. "Our friend flew off into the sky. She's a wild duck now."

For a moment, Little Duck was worried. "No, I'm not!" she said. "I'm me, I'm Little Duck. Don't you remember me?"

"Hmmm," said a rabbit friend. "She looks like Little Duck. But she can't be. Little Duck didn't want to stay here."

"Oh, no," squeaked the field mice. "Who would want to stay here for the winter?"

"Nobody, nobody, nobody," croaked the frogs.

Then they all said, "Oh no, oh no, oh no!" And suddenly, Little Duck realized they were laughing.

"Stop that!" she said. "You know I belong here. This river is my home, and you are my friends, and I am happy now."

"So are we," said her friends. "Welcome home again!"

Run! Run! Run!

Deep beneath the hot, hot sands of the desert, in a cool, cool place underground, lived a young meerkat called Kinna. Her mother had two new kits, Kip and Kambezi, and Kinna went to say hello to them.

Kinna giggled to see her brother and sister with their eyes shut tight and their hairless bodies.

"They're so still!" she said to her father.

"You were like them once," said her mother, as the babies lay snuffling her milk. "You couldn't always run like you do now."

Kinna looked pleased with herself. "I'm the fastest!" she boasted.

"Be sure to use your skill well – a life may depend on it," her father replied. Kinna sniffed with her nose in the air.

"Look at you now," continued her mother. "You're almost fully grown. I would like you to be my babysitter when your father and I have to hunt. Could you do that?"

"Course I could!" Kinna boasted. But her heart was pounding. "What an honour," she thought, "being trusted to look after the kittens."

"You wouldn't be on your own," warned her father. "The meerkat guards will be watching over you."

"Poo! Who needs them?" muttered Kinna under her breath. The day came when it was the turn of Kinna's father and mother to go off hunting. Kinna was babysitter for the day.

Her parents had told her not to take the kittens outside. But the instant they were gone, Kinna knew what she would do.

"Look at you," jested Kinna.

"You're both so pale – you need some sunshine!" and she shooed the little meerkats up the steep curves of the long tunnels.

"Run and see!" she chivvied when they reached the hole at the top, and Kip and Kambezi scrambled out onto the desert sand.

"Hot!" mumbled Kip, as she tripped and fell face down in the scratchy sand.

Kinna quickly clawed up a ball of grains and dashed them across at Kambezi and Kip.

"Uff!" Kambezi moaned, his mouth full of sand, all crunchy between his teeth.

Kinna chased her brother and sister, calling out: "Get up! Run! Run!" They chased across the desert, and without realizing it, away from the safety of the meerkat tunnels. Kinna heard the guards calling from their termite hill now far in the distance, but she wasn't trying hard enough to hear what they said.

Kinna looked up. A powerful eagle soared above, then suddenly swooped down for a better look. It was hungry, and a meerkat kitten would make a tasty meal.

The meerkat guards raced down the termite hill, stirring and swirling the sand with their claws. For a moment the eagle couldn't see the kits. Kinna raced into action, and threw sandballs at the eagle, over and over again, until one hit it right between the eyes.

"RUN!" Kinna the babysitter ordered, as Kip and Kambezi tripped in the slipping sand.

"Get up! Quick! Run!" she screeched. Kinna looked up again, and saw that the eagle had its eye on Kambezi, who had started to run in the opposite direction.

Kinna knew what she had to do. She pushed off from her back legs and pounded across the sand, grabbing Kambezi by the scruff of the neck, and running faster than she had ever run. Hot sand stung her ears and eyes, but Kinna ran for her life – and the lives of her brother and sister.

"In!" ordered the meerkat guards, as they pushed Kip, Kambezi and Kinna all at once down the entrance hole. Then the guards jumped in behind for safety. The guards would have told Kinna off for her dangerous behaviour, but the little meerkats were too busy roly-polying their way through the tunnels, in the direction of home. When they arrived, no one was there.

"I want my mummy," wailed Kip, starting to cry.

"I want my daddy," wailed Kambezi.

Kinna felt like crying too. She was the only one who realized that their parents would also be in great danger, if the eagle was still close by. But she was Kinna the babysitter. She knew she had to be brave.

So first she played a spotting game with the kittens,

. . . and then a hide-and-seek game,

. . . and then – their favourite – a chasing game.

And the kits soon forgot about being scared.

"Hello everyone!" came two warm and familiar voices along the tunnel.

"Hooray!" the kits called, as their mother and father scampered down to greet them.

"Why are you out of breath?" Mother asked, knowing from the guards that Kinna had been out with the kits.

"And why are you covered in sand?" Father asked. "Kinna?"

"We've been running," said Kip.

"In the place above," explained Kambezi.

Kinna was quiet.

Kinna's mother and father shuddered to think of their kittens in such danger. Moments earlier they themselves had been running like the wind to escape from the magnificent eagle.

But for now, Kinna helped her mother and father lull Kip and Kambezi to sleep. Together they sang the song of the wind that swept over the hot, hot sands of the desert . . .

and of a young, fearless meerkat who ran alongside.

Rapunzel

A long time ago, a man and his wife were expecting their first baby. As time passed, the wife spent much of her day resting. She would stare out of the window into a beautiful garden filled with wonderful flowers and herbs. No one ever dared to enter this garden because it was owned by a horrible witch.

One day, as the wife was looking into the garden, she noticed a clump of a delicious-looking herb. It was called rapunzel, and it looked so fresh and sweet that she could almost taste it.

In the days that followed, the woman spent more and more of her time gazing at the rapunzel. Before long, she grew quite miserable.

"What's wrong, my dear?" asked her husband.

"I want to eat the rapunzel in the witch's garden," she replied. "I think I'll be ill if I don't have some soon."

The man couldn't bear to see his wife suffer, so that night he tiptoed into the witch's garden, grabbed a bunch of rapunzel and ran back home.

His wife was overjoyed. The rapunzel tasted so delicious that she wanted more. So the next night, her husband once again tiptoed into the witch's garden. He was just about to pick the rapunzel when an ugly-looking figure jumped out at him – it was the wicked witch.

"Caught you, you thieving toad," she cackled. "You'll regret ever sneaking in here and stealing my rapunzel."

"Forgive me!" cried the man. "My wife is expecting a baby. She told me she would fall ill if she couldn't eat some of your delicious rapunzel."

"A baby, eh?" grinned the toothless witch. "Hmm! You may take as much rapunzel as you like, but you must give me your baby once it is born. If you don't

agree, I will turn you and your wife into toads."

The man had no other choice, and so he quickly agreed.

Shortly after, the woman gave birth to a beautiful baby girl. The parents were overjoyed, but their happiness was short lived. As soon as they wondered what to name her, the wicked witch appeared.

"She shall be called Rapunzel," cackled the witch. "And this will be the last time you'll ever see her." Then, with a final cackle, she took the baby and disappeared.

Rapunzel grew into a very pretty girl, with beautiful, long golden hair. When she was sixteen years old the witch locked her in a room at the top of a very tall tower. The tower had no door or stairs. The only way in was through a single window.

Every day the witch came and stood at the bottom of the tower, and called, "Rapunzel, Rapunzel, let down your fair hair."

Rapunzel would then lower her long hair through the window, and the witch would use it as a ladder.

One day, a handsome prince was riding in the woods when he heard Rapunzel singing. The prince followed the beautiful sound until he came to the tower. But, finding there was no way in, he went away. However, he was so enchanted with Rapunzel's voice that he returned to listen to her day after day.

One day, as the prince was hiding in the trees, he saw the witch arrive and call out, "Rapunzel, Rapunzel, let down your fair hair."

Then he watched in amazement as Rapunzel's golden hair tumbled to the ground and the witch climbed up into the tower. The prince waited until the witch had gone and then he went to the tower.

"Rapunzel, Rapunzel, let down your fair hair," he cried.

At once Rapunzel's hair fell to the ground and up climbed the prince. Rapunzel was afraid when she saw the prince, but his kind words soon calmed her. "I heard your beautiful voice," he explained. "Now that I've seen you, I will not rest until you agree to marry me."

Rapunzel was quite in love with the handsome prince and quickly agreed. "First, I must escape though. Bring me some silk and I will weave a ladder. Then I will be able to climb down."

So each day, after the witch had left, the prince came with silk. The witch suspected nothing until one day

Rapunzel said to the witch,

"You are so much heavier than the prince." As soon as she had said these words, Rapunzel knew she was in trouble.

"You wicked girl," screeched the witch. She grabbed a pair of scissors and cut off Rapunzel's long hair. Then she cast a spell whisking Rapunzel away to a far-off place.

That night, when the prince came to the tower, the witch was ready.

"Rapunzel, Rapunzel, let down your fair hair," called the prince. Holding on tight, the witch let Rapunzel's hair fall to the ground and up climbed the prince.

"Ahhh!" screamed the prince when the witch poked out her ugly head.

"Ha!" cried the witch. "Rapunzel's gone and you'll never set eyes on her again." Then she let go of Rapunzel's lovely locks and the prince fell to the ground. Unluckily, some rose thorns pricked his eyes and blinded him.

In the years that followed, the blind prince looked everywhere for his lost love. One day, he heard the same sweet voice he had heard before. As he wandered towards it, Rapunzel saw her handsome prince again. She ran to him weeping. The prince gathered her into his arms and her tears fell into his eyes. At once he could see again.

The prince took Rapunzel back to his kingdom, where they married and lived happily ever after.

Patrick's Monster

Patrick was excited. He was going to spend the night at his friend Sam's house. He had never been to a sleepover before, and he hoped it would be fun.

Patrick and Sam played in the garden all afternoon, and after supper they splashed in the bath for ages. By the time they were ready for bed, Patrick was really tired.

But Sam wasn't ready to go to sleep.

"We have to check under our

beds first," he told Patrick.

"Why?" asked Patrick, puzzled.

"In case there are monsters," said Sam. "Monsters sometimes live under people's beds!"

Sam looked very worried, so Patrick started to worry too.

"My mum says there's no such thing as monsters," he said to Sam. But he didn't feel too certain.

"My mum says that too," said Sam, "but grown-ups don't know everything! We have to look."

Patrick and Sam looked under both beds, very carefully. There was nothing but a ball of dust under Patrick's bed, and two plastic bricks under Sam's.

"It's okay," said Sam. "It's safe to go to sleep now."

But Patrick still felt worried, and it took him a long time to fall asleep.

In the morning, the idea of monsters didn't seem frightening any more. By lunchtime, when his mum came to collect him, Patrick had forgotten all about what Sam had said.

But that night, after his mum had tucked him in and read his favourite bedtime story, Patrick remembered. And he got worried all over again. What if there was a monster under his bed?

Patrick was too worried to go to sleep. He had to look under his bed and check for monsters.

Slowly and quietly, Patrick crawled out from under the covers and crouched down beside his bed. Then, holding his breath, he bent down, looked under the bed, and saw . . .

two BIG eyes staring back at him!

Patrick gasped and jumped back. Then he looked again, just to make sure he hadn't dreamed it.

Sure enough, there were two big eyes looking at him. But they weren't scary eyes. They were warm, friendly eyes, and when Patrick looked a little harder, he could see that they were part of a face – a monster face! But it was a fuzzy, friendly monster face, and it was smiling at him.

"Hello," Patrick whispered.

"Hello," came the reply.

"Who are you?" Patrick asked.

"I'm Marvin," said the monster. "I live here, under your bed."

"I'm Patrick," said Patrick.

"I know," said Marvin. "I've been waiting ever so long for you to find me. I had almost given up hope!"

"Would you like to come out from under there?" Patrick asked.

"I thought you'd never ask!" said Marvin happily, as he shuffled out into the middle of the room.

Patrick could see now that Marvin was fat and round and fuzzy all over. And he was purple! Purple was Patrick's favourite colour!

"How long have you been under my bed?" he asked.

"Days and days and days!" said Marvin. "And it's

been very lonely. And scary, too!"

Patrick was amazed that a monster could be scared.

"What were you scared of?" he asked Marvin.

"I was scared that you might never find me, and I'd always be alone," said Marvin. "Monsters need friends too, you know!"

Patrick and Marvin raced Patrick's cars around the room. Then Marvin taught Patrick his special romping, stomping, creeping, leaping, merry monster dance. They were having so much fun they didn't hear Patrick's mum coming up the stairs.

"What on earth is going on here?" asked Mum, opening the door.

"I was just playing with my . . . er . . . new friend," said Patrick. He looked down at Marvin, who was sitting at his feet as still and silent as an empty slipper.

"What a cute cuddly toy!" said Mum. "Now it's time for bed," she said, tucking Patrick up with Marvin. "Night-night."

"Night-night, Mum," said Patrick. "Night-night, Marvin Monster," he said, when Mum had gone.

"Night-night," whispered Marvin. "Thank you for rescuing me from under the bed."

"Thank you for being my friend," said Patrick. And as he drifted into sweet monster dreams, Patrick knew that he would never worry about monsters again.

Boys and Girls Come Out to Play

Boys and girls come out to play,
The moon doth shine as bright as day.
Leave your supper and leave your sleep,
And join your playfellows in the street.

Come with a whoop and come with a call,
Come with a good will or not at all.
Up the ladder and down the wall,
A halfpenny loaf will serve us all.
You find milk, and I'll find flour,
And we'll have a pudding in half an hour.

Goosey, Goosey, Gander

Goosey, goosey, gander,
Whither shall I wander?
Upstairs and downstairs
And in my lady's chamber.
There I met an old man
Who would not say his prayers,
So I took him by the left leg
And threw him down the stairs.